ABHINANDAN PATIL

Learning Python Through LAB Based Approach

Copyright © 2023 by Abhinandan Patil

All rights reserved. No part of this publication may be reproduced, stored or transmitted in any form or by any means, electronic, mechanical, photocopying, recording, scanning, or otherwise without written permission from the publisher. It is illegal to copy this book, post it to a website, or distribute it by any other means without permission.

First edition

This book was professionally typeset on Reedsy. Find out more at reedsy.com

To My Wife Sangeeta and Kids Ishan and Shivansh

There is no alternative to hard-work and perseverance.

— Abhinandan H. Patil

Contents

Preface	ii
Acknowledgement	iii
About the Author, Me	iv
Introduction to Python	1
Program 1	2
Program 2	4
Program 3	6
Program 4	8
Program 5	10
Program 6	13
Program 7	15
Program 8	17
Program 9	18
Program 10	20
Program 11	21
Program 12	22
Program 13	24
Program 14	25
Program 15	27
Program 16	29
Program 17	32
Program 18	34
Program 19	37
Program 20	39

Preface

This book is totally informal and unconventional in its approach. Theory text is kept bare minimal. Targeted readers of this book are novice Python programmers. Author mentions about some Authoritative books by other competent Authors for beginners. The Author takes application of learned concepts approach . This book contains close to 20 practical problems and their solutions. Author liberally uses his own notes that he used for teaching at Universities. The Author strongly asserts his copyright over every content in this book that he prepared for teaching. This book is lab oriented and tests you on your learned concepts. After solving all the problems you should have gained some knowledge in Python. The intention of these book is to help novice learner. Good luck!.

Acknowledgement

First of all many thanks to Reedsy for giving me a software where type setting and formatting is breeze. Many Thanks to Microsoft Corporation for the wonderful OS Windows 11 with add on utilities. Also thanks to Microsoft
Corporation and Open source community for VSCode and its extensions. Python extensions in VSCode are amazing. Many Thanks to Python communities. Applications such as Okular, Snipping Tool were very handy. Dell Corporation and HP need a mention for giving wonderful hardware. Finally Author thanks other Authors whose material is readily available for Python learners.

About the Author, Me

I am a proud global citizen and published teacher with 3 Udemy courses, 15 Books, open access Blog and open access YouTube channel. I can teach Computational Mathematics, Data Science, ML/DL, Internet of Things, Programming languages, Web technologies, Cloud Computing, Microcontrollers, Electronics for Computer Scientists, Operating Systems, Computer Networks, Data Structures and Algorithms, Software Engineering and Software Testing. I am Author of 15 Books and 14 Scientific Articles. I am Life-Long learner with many areas of interests. Earlier, I have worked in Wireless Network Software Organization as Lead Software Engineer for close to a decade. I was in USA for two long stints and was instrumental in Releases of Mobility Manager at Motorola USA as Single Point of Contact for Network Simulator Tool. My Research is available as Books and Thesis in IJSER, USA. My Thesis published as Book is rated as one of the best Books of all time for Regression testing by BookAuthority.org. I am an Active Researcher in the field of Computational Mathematics, Machine Learning, Deep Learning, Data Science, Artificial Intelligence, Regression Testing applied to Networks, Communication and Internet of Things. I am an active contributor of Science, Technology, Engineering and Mathematics. I am currently working on few Undisclosed Books. I have started Blogging recently on Technology and Allied Areas. I have been National and International awardee. I am Senior IEEE member since 2013 and member of Smart Tribe and Cheeky Scientists Association. I am UGC-NET Qualified (2012). Recipient of several Bravo awards for deserving work at Motorola. I am on the Editorial Board of few Scientific Journals. I am an ardent reader of STEM(Science, Technology, Engineering and Mathematics). I have desire to contribute more to STEM. More details about me at: https://abhinandanhpatil.info/

Introduction to Python

Python is probably the most used language because of its rich libraries ranging from Scipy, Sympy for Scientific and Mathematical Programming to Flask, Django for Web backend programming to Scikit learn and Keras+Tensorflow for Machine Learning and Deep Learning. Already Python is documented by many Authoritative Authors including:

1. Python Tutorial Release 3.8.3 by Guido Van Rossum and Python Development team.
2. Beginning Python by Magnus Lie Hetland
3. Think Python by Allen B. Downey
4. Python Essential Reference by David M. Beazley
5. Python Cookbook by David Beazley and Brian K. Jones

Many good Python courses in Udemy and other portals. Following Git Hub repository for Python are working relentlessly to make Python popular
   url = https://github.com/vinta/awesome-python
   url = https://github.com/realpython/materials.git

Program 1

Write a python program to find the best of two test average marks out of three test's marks accepted from the user.

```python
'''
Program 1
Write a python program to find the best of two test average marks
out of three test's
marks accepted from the user.
'''

def list_avg(test_marks):
    return sum(test_marks)/ len(test_marks)

def give_best_two(test_marks):
    return_list = []
    test_marks.sort(reverse=True)
    return_list.append(test_marks[0])
    return_list.append(test_marks[1])
    return return_list

def function_main():
    passed_list = []
    return_list = []
    first_test_marks = int(input('Enter the first test marks'))
    second_test_marks = int(input('Enter the second test marks'))
    third_test_marks = int(input('Enter the third test marks'))
    passed_list.append(first_test_marks)
```

PROGRAM 1

```
    passed_list.append(second_test_marks)
    passed_list.append(third_test_marks)
    return_list = give_best_two(passed_list)
    avg_of_best_two = list_avg(return_list)
    print("You passed marks
    :",first_test_marks,",",second_test_marks,",",third_test_marks,"")
    print("Best two",return_list)
    print("Average of best two tests is",avg_of_best_two)

if __name__=='__main__':
    print(__doc__)
    function_main()
```

Program 2

Develop a Python program to check whether a given number is palindrome or not and also count the number of occurrences of each digit in the input number.

```
'''
Program 2
Develop a Python program to check whether a given number is
palindrome or not and
also count the number of occurrences of each digit in the input
number.
'''

def count_occurrences_of_digits(num):
  dictionary = {0:0,1:0,2:0,3:0,4:0,5:0,6:0,7:0,8:0,9:0}
  temp = num
  while(temp > 0):
    dig=temp % 10
    dictionary[dig] = dictionary[dig] + 1
    temp = temp//10
  return dictionary

def is_palindrome(num):
  temp=num
  rev=0
  while(num>0):
    dig=num%10
    rev=rev*10+dig
```

PROGRAM 2

```python
        num=num//10
    if(temp==rev):
        return True
    else:
        return False

def function_main():
    digits_in_decimal = 10
    num=int(input("Enter number:"))
    num_is_palindrome = is_palindrome(num)
    if(num_is_palindrome):
        print("It is a palindrome")
    else:
        print("It is NOT a palindrome")
    retuned_dictionary = count_occurrences_of_digits(num)
    for i in range(digits_in_decimal):
        print(i,"Occured",retuned_dictionary[i],"times")

if __name__=='__main__':
    print(__doc__)
    function_main()
```

Program 3

Define a function F as Fn = Fn-1 + Fn-2. Write a Python program which accepts a value for N (where N >0) as input and pass this value to the function. Display suitable error message if the condition for input value is not followed.

```python
'''
Program 3
Defined as a function F as Fn = Fn-1 + Fn-2. Write a Python
program which accepts a
value for N (where N >0) as input and pass this value to the
function. Display suitable
error message if the condition for input value is not followed.
'''

def nth_term_of_fibonnaci(n):
  if n <= 1:
    return n
  else:
    return(nth_term_of_fibonnaci(n-1) + nth_term_of_fibonnaci(n-2))


def main_function():
  nterms = int(input("Enter number of terms of Fibonacci "))
  if nterms <= 0:
    print("Plese enter a positive integer")
  else:
    print("Fibonacci sequence:")
    for i in range(nterms):
```

PROGRAM 3

```
        print(nth_term_of_fibonnaci(i), end=' ')

if __name__=='__main__':
  print(__doc__)
  main_function()
```

Program 4

Develop a python program to convert binary to decimal, octal to hexadecimal using functions.

```
'''
Program 4
Develop a python program to convert binary to decimal, octal to
hexadecimal using
functions
'''
def binary_to_decimal(binary):
    binary1 = binary
    decimal, i, n = 0, 0, 0
    while(binary != 0):
        dec = binary % 10
        decimal = decimal + dec * pow(2, i)
        binary = binary//10
        i += 1
    print(decimal)


def octal_to_hex(octal):
    octal1 = octal
    decimal, i, n = 0, 0, 0
    while(octal != 0):
        dec = octal % 10
        decimal = decimal + dec * pow(8, i)
```

PROGRAM 4

```
        octal = octal//10
        i += 1
    print(hex(decimal))


def function_main():
    entered_binary_value = int(input("Enter the binary value in
    string format"))
    entered_octal_value = int(input("Enter the octal value in string
    format"))

    binary_to_decimal(entered_binary_value)
    octal_to_hex(entered_octal_value)
    return

if __name__=='__main__':
    print(__doc__)
    function_main()
```

Program 5

Write a Python program that accepts a sentence and find the number of words, digits, uppercase letters and lowercase letters. Write a Python program to find the string similarity between two given strings

```
'''
Program 5
 Write a Python program that accepts a sentence and find the
 number of words, digits,
uppercase letters and lowercase letters.
3.b
Write a Python program to find the string similarity between two
given strings
'''
from difflib import SequenceMatcher

def similarity_ratio_between_two_strings(string1,string2):
    print("Entered Strings are:",string1,"and:",string2)
    print("Similarity ratio between two strings :", end="")
    print(SequenceMatcher(None, string1, string2).ratio())
    return

def string_test(s):
    d={"UPPER_CASE":0, "LOWER_CASE":0,"DIGITS":0,"WORDCOUNT":0}

    upper_case = []
    lower_case = []
    digits = []
```

PROGRAM 5

```python
  for c in s:
    if c.isupper():
      d["UPPER_CASE"]+=1
      upper_case.append(c)
    elif c.islower():
      d["LOWER_CASE"]+=1
      lower_case.append(c)
    elif c.isdigit():
      d["DIGITS"]+=1
      digits.append(c)
    elif c.isspace():
      d["WORDCOUNT"]+=1
    else:
      pass
  print ("Entered String : ", s)
  print ("No. of Upper case characters : ", d["UPPER_CASE"])
  print ("No. of Lower case Characters : ", d["LOWER_CASE"])
  print ("No. of digits :", d["DIGITS"])
  print ("No. of words : ", d["WORDCOUNT"]+1)
  print("Upper case characters",upper_case)
  print("Lower case characters",lower_case)
  print("DIGITS characters",digits)
  return

def main_function():
  print("===== Menu ===========")
  print("1. String Statistics")
  print("2. String Similarity")
  print("Enter 1 or 2")
  print("==========================")
  choice = int(input())
  if choice != 1 and choice != 2:
    print("Please enter 1 or 2 only")
  if choice == 1:
    input_str = input("Enter the input string whos statistics you
    want ")
    string_test(input_str)
  elif choice == 2:
    string1 = input("Enter the first string")
```

```
        string2 = input("Enter the second string")
        similarity_ratio_between_two_strings(string1,string2)
    return


if __name__=='__main__':
    print(__doc__)
    main_function()
```

Program 6

Write a python program to implement insertion sort and merge sort using lists

```
'''
Program 6
Write a python program to implement insertion sort and merge sort
using lists
'''

import time
import random
comparison,swaps = 0,0

# Nearly Brute Force
def insertion_sort_old(unsorted_list):
    global comparison
    global swaps
    for i in range(len(unsorted_list)):
        j = i + 1
        for j in range(len(unsorted_list)):
            comparison+=1
            if unsorted_list[i] < unsorted_list[j]:
                swaps+= 1
                temp = unsorted_list[i]
                unsorted_list[i] = unsorted_list[j]
                unsorted_list[j] = temp
    print(comparison,"Comparisons and", swaps, "Swaps")
```

```
    return

randomlist = random.sample(range(0, 50), 50)
data = randomlist.copy()
print("Unsorted list",data)
insertion_sort_old(data)
print('Sorted list in Ascending Order:')
print(data)
```

Program 7

Python implementation of the merge sort algorithm

```
"""
Taken from url = https://github.com/TheAlgorithms/Python.git

MIT License

This is a pure Python implementation of the merge sort algorithm

"""
import random
def merge_sort(collection):

    def merge(left, right):

        result = []
        while left and right:

            result.append((left if left[0] <= right[0] else
            right).pop(0))
        return result + left + right

    if len(collection) <= 1:
        return collection
    mid = len(collection) // 2
    return merge(merge_sort(collection[:mid]),
    merge_sort(collection[mid:]))
```

```
def function_main():


    unsorted = random.sample(range(0, 50), 50)
    print("Unsorted: ",unsorted)
    sorted_list = merge_sort(unsorted)
    print("Sorted: ",sorted_list)
    #print(merge_sort(unsorted), sep=",")

function_main()
```

Program 8

Write a program to convert roman numbers in to integer values using dictionaries.

```
class py_solution:
    def roman_to_int(self, s):
        rom_val = {'I': 1, 'V': 5, 'X': 10, 'L': 50, 'C': 100, 'D':
        500, 'M': 1000}
        int_val = 0
        for i in range(len(s)):
            if i > 0 and rom_val[s[i]] > rom_val[s[i - 1]]:
                int_val += rom_val[s[i]] - 2 * rom_val[s[i - 1]]
            else:
                int_val += rom_val[s[i]]
        return int_val

print(py_solution().roman_to_int('IV'))
print(py_solution().roman_to_int('VII'))
print(py_solution().roman_to_int('MMMCMLXXXVI'))
print(py_solution().roman_to_int('MMMM'))
print(py_solution().roman_to_int('C'))
```

Program 9

Write a function called isphonenumber () to recognize a pattern 415-555-4242 without using regular expression and also write the code to recognize the same pattern using regular expression.

```
'''
Program 9
  Write a function called isphonenumber () to recognize a pattern
  415-555-4242 without
using regular expression and also write the code to recognize the
same pattern using
regular expression.
'''

def isPhoneNumber(text):
  if len(text) != 12:
    return False
  for i in range(0, 3):
    if not text[i].isdecimal():
      return False
  if text[3] != '-':
    return False
  for i in range(4, 7):
    if not text[i].isdecimal():
        return False
  if text[7] != '-':
    return False
  for i in range(8, 12):
```

PROGRAM 9

```
    if not text[i].isdecimal():
        return False
    return True

print('Is 415-555-4242 a phone number?')
print(isPhoneNumber('415-555-4242'))
print('Is Moshi moshi a phone number?')
print(isPhoneNumber('Moshi moshi'))
```

Program 10

Write a function called isphonenumber () to recognize a pattern 415-555-4242 without using regular expression and also write the code to recognize the same pattern using regular expression.

```
'''
Program 10
  Write a function called isphonenumber () to recognize a pattern
  415-555-4242 without
using regular expression and also write the code to recognize the
same pattern using
regular expression.
'''
import re

phoneNumRegex = re.compile(r'\d\d\d-\d\d\d-\d\d\d\d')
mo = phoneNumRegex.search('My number is 415-555-4242.')
print('Phone number found: ' + mo.group())

print(phoneNumRegex.findall('Cell: 415-555-9999 Work: 212-555-0000'))
```

Program 11

Develop a python program that could search the text in a file for phone numbers (+919900889977) and email addresses (sample@gmail.com)

```
'''
Program 11
Develop a python program that could search the text in a file for
phone numbers
(+919900889977) and email addresses (sample@gmail.com)
'''

import re

phoneNumRegex = re.compile(r'\+\d\d\d\d\d\d\d\d\d\d\d\d')
emailRegex = re.compile(r'\w+\@\w+\.\w+')

mo = phoneNumRegex.search('(+919900889977) is my mobile number')
print(mo.group())

em = emailRegex.search('Abhinandan@gmail.com is my email address')
print(em.group())
```

Program 12

Write a python program to accept a file name from the user and perform the following operations

1. Display the first N line of the file
2. Find the frequency of occurrence of the word accepted from the user in the file

```python
'''
Program 12
Write a python program to accept a file name from the user and
perform the following
operations
1. Display the first N line of the file
2. Find the frequency of occurrence of the word accepted from the
user in the
file
'''


def count_occurrences_of_given_word(file_to_be_searched,
passed_word):
    passed_word_count = 0

    text = open(file_to_be_searched, "r")
```

```python
    for line in text:
        line = line.strip()
        words = line.split(" ")

        for word in words:

            if word == passed_word:

                passed_word_count+=1
    print("Given word",passed_word,"occurrences
    is",passed_word_count)

def file_read_desired_lines(file_to_be_searched,
line_count_desired):
    f = open(file_to_be_searched, "r")
    print("First" ,line_count_desired,"lines are as follows")
    for i in range(line_count_desired):
        print(f.readline())

def function_main():
    file_to_be_searched = input("Enter the file to be searched: ")
    word_to_be_searched = input("Enter the word to be searched: ")
    desired_line_count = int(input("How many lines to be printed: "))
    count_occurrences_of_given_word(file_to_be_searched,word_to_be_searched)
    file_read_desired_lines(file_to_be_searched,desired_line_count)

if __name__=='__main__':
    function_main()
```

Program 13

Write a python program to create a ZIP file of a particular folder which contains several files inside it.

```python
'''
Program 13
Write a python program to create a ZIP file of a particular folder
which contains several files inside it.
'''

import os
import shutil
from zipfile import ZipFile
from os import path
from shutil import make_archive

def main_function():
    archive_name = os.path.expanduser(os.path.join('.', 'myarchive'))
    root_dir = os.path.expanduser(os.path.join('.', 'pdf_files'))
    if not os.path.isdir(root_dir):
        print('Not a valid directory for archive')
    make_archive(archive_name, 'zip', root_dir)

if __name__=='__main__':
    print(__doc__)
    main_function()
```

Program 14

By using the concept of inheritance write a python program to find the area of triangle, circle and rectangle.

```
'''
Program 14
By using the concept of inheritance write a python program to find
the area of triangle,
circle and rectangle.
'''


import math

class shape:

    def __init__(self):
        self.calc_area = 0


class triangle(shape):

    def __init__(self, a, b, c):
        self.a=a
        self.b=b
        self.c=c

    def area(self):
```

```python
        s=(self.a+self.b+self.c)/2
        calc_area=math.sqrt(s*(s-self.a)*(s-self.b)*(s-self.c))
        return calc_area

class circle(shape):

    def __init__(self,r):
        self.r = r

    def area(self):
        self.calc_area = math.pi * self.r**2
        return self.calc_area

class rectangle(shape):

    def __init__(self,b,h):
        self.b = b
        self.h = h

    def area(self):
        self.calc_area = self.b*self.h
        return self.calc_area

def function_main():

    t1=triangle(4,13,15)
    c1=circle(5)
    r1=rectangle(5,6)
    print("Area of rectangle is",t1.area())
    print("Area of circle is",c1.area())
    print("Area of rectangle is",r1.area())

if __name__=='__main__':
    print(__doc__)
    function_main()
```

Program 15

Write a python program by creating a class called Employee to store the details of Name, Employee_ID, Department and Salary, and implement a method to update salary of employees belonging to a given department.

```python
'''
Program 15
Write a python program by creating a class called Employee to
store the details of
Name, Employee_ID, Department and Salary, and implement a method
to update salary
of employees belonging to a given department.
'''
class employee:
    def __init__(self):
        __id = 0
        __name = ""
        __gender = ""
        __city = ""
        __salary = 0

    def set_data(self, id=0, name=" ",gender = "", city = "", salary =0):
        self.__id=id
        self.__name = name
        self.__gender = gender
        self.__city = city
```

```python
        self.__salary = salary


    def display_employee_data(self):
        print("-------------------------")
        print("Id\t:",self.__id)
        print("Name\t:", self.__name)
        print("Gender\t:", self.__gender)
        print("City\t:", self.__city)
        print("Salary\t:", self.__salary)
        print("-------------------------")

def main_function():
    emp=employee()
    emp.set_data(1,'ramy','male','hyderabad',55000)
    emp.display_employee_data()
    emp.set_data(1,'ramy','male','hyderabad',70000)
    emp.display_employee_data()
    emp1 = employee()
    emp1.set_data(2,'reddy','male','hyderabad',66000)
    emp1.display_employee_data()

if __name__=='__main__':
    print(__doc__)
    main_function()
```

Program 16

Write a python program to find the whether the given input is palindrome or not (for both string and integer) using the concept of polymorphism and inheritance.

```python
'''
Program 16
 Write a python program to find the whether the given input is
 palindrome or not (for
both string and integer) using the concept of polymorphism and
inheritance.
'''
import math

class number:

    def __init__(self):
        self.stored_value = 0

    def check_palindrome(self):
        pass


class palindrome(number):

    def __init__(self, passed_number):
        self.stored_value= passed_number
```

```python
    def check_palindrome(self):
      num=self.stored_value
      rev=0
      while(num>0):
        dig=num%10
        rev=rev*10+dig
        num=num//10
      if(self.stored_value==rev):
        print("It is palindrome")
      else:
        print("It is not palindrome")

class palindrome_string_input(number):

  def __init__(self,passed_string):
    self.stored_value = passed_string

  def check_palindrome(self):
    num=int(self.stored_value)
    rev=0
    while(num>0):
      dig=num%10
      rev=rev*10+dig
      num=num//10
    if(int(self.stored_value)==rev):
      print("It is palindrome")
    else:
      print("It is not palindrome")


def function_main():
  base_num = number()
  test_num = palindrome(12121)
  base_num = test_num
  base_num.check_palindrome()
  test_num1 = palindrome(12122)
  base_num = test_num1
  base_num.check_palindrome()
```

PROGRAM 16

```
    string_num = palindrome_string_input("12121")
    base_num = string_num
    base_num.check_palindrome()
    string_num1 = palindrome_string_input("12131")
    base_num = string_num1
    base_num.check_palindrome()

if __name__=='__main__':
    print(__doc__)
    function_main()
```

Program 17

Write a python program to download the all XKCD comics

```python
'''
Program 17
Write a python program to download the all XKCD comics
'''

import requests as req
import os, bs4
import json


base_url = 'https://xkcd.com/'
os.makedirs('xkcd', exist_ok=True)
entered_num = input("Input the comic number example 1414: ")
base_url += entered_num
print('Downloading image from location ----' ,base_url)
res = req.get(base_url)
soup = bs4.BeautifulSoup(res.text,"html.parser")
comic_elem = soup.select('#comic img')
comic_url = 'http:' + comic_elem[0].get('src')
print("comic_url is: "+comic_url)

res = req.get(comic_url)

image_file = open(os.path.join('xkcd',
os.path.basename(comic_url)), 'wb')
```

PROGRAM 17

```
for data_chunk in res.iter_content():
    image_file.write(data_chunk)
image_file.close()
print('Downloaded the image file to
location',os.path.join('xkcd'),"File name
is",os.path.basename(comic_url))
```

Program 18

Demonstrate python program to read the data from the spreadsheet and write the data in to the spreadsheet

```
'''
Program 18
Demonstrate python program to read the data from the spreadsheet
and write the data in to the spreadsheet
'''
import pandas as pd
from pandas import DataFrame

df1 = pd.read_excel('Book1.xlsx')

print(df1)

#df2 = pd.DataFrame({"5":[6, "GH", 33, "EC", 45],"6":[7, "IJ", 37, "CS", 90]})

df2 = pd.DataFrame({"SI. NO":[ 6, 7],
                    "Name":["GH","IJ"],
                    "Age" : [33,37],
                    "Stream": ["EC","CS"],
                    "Percentage":[45,90]})

df_concat = pd.concat([df1, df2], ignore_index=True,axis=0)
```

PROGRAM 18

```
df_concat.to_excel("Book2.xlsx")

dataframe4 = pd.read_excel("Book2.xlsx")

print(dataframe4)
```

Pre-requisites

	A	B	C	D	E	F	G
1	Sl. NO	Name	Age	Stream	Percentage		
2	1	AB	18	EC	50		
3	2	BC	19	CS	90		
4	3	CD	20	ME	70		
5	4	DE	21	IP	56		
6	5	EF	22	EE	65		

After execution:

	A	B	C	D	E	F
1		Sl. NO	Name	Age	Stream	Percentage
2	0	1	AB	18	EC	50
3	1	2	BC	19	CS	90
4	2	3	CD	20	ME	70
5	3	4	DE	21	IP	56
6	4	5	EF	22	EE	65
7	5	6	GH	33	EC	45
8	6	7	IJ	37	CS	90

Program 19

Write a python program to combine pages from many PDFs

```
'''
Program 19
 Write a python program to combine pages from many PDFs
'''

from PyPDF2 import PdfFileMerger

#Create and instance of PdfFileMerger() class
merger = PdfFileMerger()

#Create a list with file names
pdf_files = ['pdf_files/sample_page1.pdf',
'pdf_files/sample_page2.pdf']

#Iterate over the list of file names
for pdf_file in pdf_files:
    #Append PDF files
    merger.append(pdf_file)

#Write out the merged PDF
merger.write("merged_2_pages.pdf")
merger.close()
```

Pre-requisites:

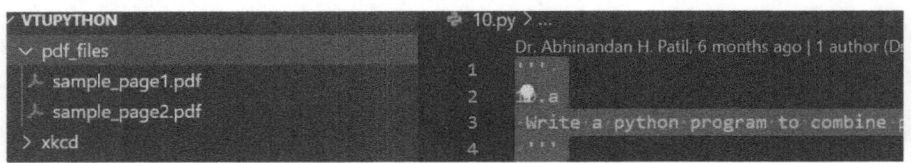

After execution:

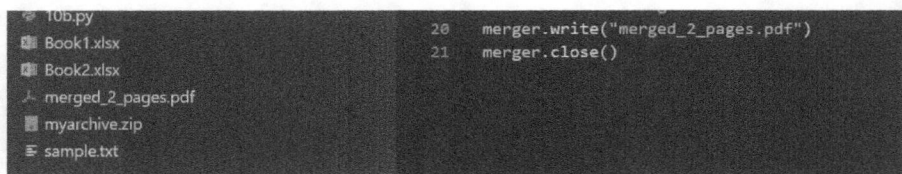

Program 20

Write a python program to fetch current weather data from the JSON file

```
'''
Program 20
Write a python program to fetch current weather data from the JSON
file
'''
import requests, json

api_key = "Replace this with Your API Key"

base_url = "http://api.openweathermap.org/data/2.5/weather?"

#https://api.openweathermap.org/data/2.5/weather?q=London&appid=360396a690bbda

entered_city = input("Enter city name : ")

complete_url = base_url + "q=" + entered_city +"&appid=" + api_key

response = requests.get(complete_url)

x = response.json()


if x["cod"] != "404":
```

```
        temperature = x["main"]["temp"]
        pressure = x["main"]["pressure"]
        humidity = x["main"]["humidity"]
        weather = x["weather"]
        weather_description = weather[0]["description"]
        print('\033[1m' + "Weather description is:
        "+str(weather_description) + '\033[0m')
        print("Additional Weather description is follows:\n")
        print("\n\n Temparature is = " +
                str(temperature) +
           "\n Atmospheric pressure = " +
                str(pressure) +
           "\n Humidity = " +
                str(humidity))
else:
    print(" Please enter valid city name ")
```

www.ingramcontent.com/pod-product-compliance
Lightning Source LLC
Chambersburg PA
CBHW072259170526
45158CB00003BA/1112